Tethered

A Collection of Intimate Poems

Cissy Stag

Tethered

Dedication

For you...

(You know who you are.)

I don't have to see you get better to know that you are trying... but it's a privilege to witness.

Introduction

Hi. I'm Cissy. I started writing this book while marketing my debut book *Stripped: A Collection of Poems Written in Recovery.*

Stripped was a collection of poems written from the heart, and... *Stripped* became a powerful tool for me to use on social media to regain my power.

Poetry helped me recover from my psychotic episode and an aftermath that I wouldn't wish on my worst enemies... even though they caused it.

As I began writing *Tethered,* I experienced intense internal psychological warfare between Cissy the person and Cissy the entertainer. I learned the dark art of manipulation to survive, and it had a lasting impact on my psyche. Every social interaction was plagued by my crisis of identity after I cast myself into the role of the perfect villain. It made connecting with others extraordinarily difficult.

Tethered is an exploration of my feelings of being larger than life... otherworldly... grandiose... and intentionally channeling my feelings into imaginative spaces so that I can stay tethered to reality. The reality is this: I am worthy of love, compassion, and community... as are those who hurt me.

Table of Contents

"Artificial"

A sequel...

Seems silly.

Stripped has been out for a week!

But I'm still not healed...

Still not rich.

Still not famous.

And still making enemies of people I once called friends.

I find myself sliding back into old habits.

Replaying old memories.

Same cycle.

Different product.

What do you when all you have is writing?

And now the cover art is the controversy?

Every day, I feel closer to the woman on the cover.

Built with technology.

Or magic.

An illusion.

A mirage.

Eye-catching.

Intelligent.

But artificial...

And ready to burn the mortal world to the ground.

"Intuition"

I love you.

There.

I said it.

Again.

I love you.

I hate you.

But I can't be indifferent to you.

Trust...

Ha!

But seriously... trust me,

And I'll trust you.

Because we are better off apart...

Dancer.

Artist.

Empath.

Creator...

Creature of the night...

I recognized you in the woods... and you recognized me... but I don't think that you were able to believe your eyes at the time.

I love you.

I hate you.

I trust you...

Please...

Trust me.

"Grandiose"

I don't feel like a person anymore.

I feel like a God.

I must be a God to have danced with The Devil...

If I am, in fact, not The Devil myself.

I'm uncertain.

I don't feel like a person.

How could I?

I learned the art of psychological warfare to extinguish the blaze that burned me alive...

And it sparked a new war in my mind...

One that has me second guessing my intentions...

My character.

My morals.

My values...

Machiavellianism.

Gain power.

By any means necessary...

Am I sure that it is better to be feared than to be loved?

I feel like a God,

But I'm not a God.

And you're not The Devil.

I say it...

But I'm not sure that I believe it.

I fear that I may be losing my tether to reality.

"Celeste"

Celeste.

Because I must let you go.

So that I can heal.

For my safety.

For my sanity.

For my happiness.

Celeste.

Because I am still infatuated with the ghost of you.

Inhale.

I love the scent of smoke...

From your flame burning bright and Blue.

Celeste.

Because the shadow you cast is heavenly.

I'm under your spell.

Celeste.

Because we can't be together,

But maybe we were in our last lives...

Or maybe we will be in our next...

Celeste.

Because I want to protect you.

I want to shield you from the cruel world that you do not yet know.

Celeste.

Because I think...

I know...

We are star-crossed.

"Imaginary"

It wasn't supposed to be like this...

You were never supposed to be a fictional character in my life,

But now you are.

I'm teetering the line between fact and fiction...

Because the fact is that you hurt me.

You stripped me of my power.

You stripped me of my voice.

And now I must ask a higher power to get involved...

To ensure that you stop,

And to ensure that you never take my power again.

Celeste is a ghost of you.

Celeste is my reflection.

Celeste is a character.

An imaginary friend for the adult woman...

Because Celeste keeps me tethered to this world,

To the truth,

And Celeste keeps me safe.

"Fiction"

I cannot believe that I am writing a book dedicated to a fictional character,

But is it really any different than when I wrote a book dedicated to real people?

Because actions showed me their real character...

But my view of them when I hurt the most was always fiction.

"Risk"

The risk of being hated by you is not worth the reward of being loved by you.

"Guardian"

It's me.

Your Guardian Demon.

Hi.

I'm writing you while gazing up from Hell.

I see you.

Full of light.

Full of darkness.

And in dire need of a break.

Step into your power.

But before you do that,

Step back.

Breathe.

Inhale.

Exhale.

I walked in your shoes not long ago,

And it was frightening.

But you will be okay.

Hell will always be here waiting for you.

Until your time,

Breathe the air of the mortal world when it rains.

Submerge yourself in spaces where you feel weightless.

And give yourself time.

Life is short,

But it's shorter if you burn out.

So, burn slowly.

Bright.

And Blue.

"Forgive Me (Reprise)"

You wished me dead.

The detail that I must fixate on through every decision.

I wished you well...

And you wished me dead...

If I lie and say that I love you,

Will you let me go?

No?

Well, what if I hate you?

Is that enough to repel you?

What if I am indifferent to you?

Would you believe that?

Grow bored?

Fixate on another?

If I lie and say that I love you,

Will that make you happy?

Enough to let sleeping hounds lie...?

It's never enough.

Not this way.

Or that way.

And that's why I said goodbye.

Good riddance.

And have a good life.

I value your humanity...

But you are not a person worthy of my respect.

I'm done.

With the lies told for your comfort.

You wished me dead...

Forgive me...

For I cannot forgive you for the words that you said.

"The Surface"

Inhale.

Exhale.

I'm at the surface of the water.

Floating.

Face up.

My hair is stiff with salt.

And I haven't made it to the shore.

But I made it to the surface.

From the bottom of the ocean.

"Sad, Beautiful Man"

A first...

In a long time.

A man in my bed...

Sad, and beautiful.

I think about writing as I watch his tired eyes drift shut.

His heart aches in a way that is all too familiar to me.

I am left speechless.

I fear that he's going to be a problem for me...

Intense.

All-consuming.

In every way that I want.

I cannot believe my eyes.

He rests so peacefully through his chaos.

I hope that he stays peaceful.

I don't know what I can offer later...

But now... I want to offer him peace...

Because he offers me comfort.

"Attached"

He says that he gets attached.

I do, too.

This initially brought me comfort.

But today it brings me fear.

Because what if he doesn't get attached like I do?

Inhale & exhale every scent of him in my presence.

All-consuming attachment.

The kind that makes you fall in love quickly.

DEEPLY.

And breaks your heart in the end.

Is it worth the risk?

...I hope so.

I remember when it was all about her,

And before her, it was all about him...

And before him... it was all about them.

Every fiber of my being wants him now.

Desperate for distraction and aching with attraction.

DAMN... I'm impatient.

He's beautiful.

I never thought I'd feel that way about a man after my last.

"Stars"

What if you're in love with me?

But it doesn't matter...

What if you're in love with me?

But you're too afraid to approach...

And I... can't...

What if you hate me?

But you're in love with me?

And for those reasons, you're never sure?

Unwilling to sacrifice your stability to find out?

What if these feelings aren't yours?

What if they are mine?

Because... I just... hate you that much...

And love you that much...

That I don't want you to know instability like mine.

What if we're in love?

And it never matters?

Because our love is never safe.

Never stable.

Never trustworthy...

What if the stars align...

And we don't trust them?

Because we're of this place.

This earth.

And the stars are beautiful...

But what if that's all that they are?

"Green"

Meet me in the Green

Below the stones

Where water flows into the deep

Nurturing every living thing at the bottom

Find me seated where the creek trickles.

Surrounded by trees.

Where the city disappears.

Embrace me in the shade.

Under the canopy.

In a place private and safe.

Like the water that soars to the bottom,

I know that I will fall.

Rapidly.

I always do.

Watch me brace for impact...

As I take the leap.

Because even if I crash into oblivion,

The fall is worth the excitement.

"Central America"

When you know, you know.

Meet me in ATL.

Next decade.

Where the planes come and go.

Let's take a trip.

To Central America.

When you know, you know,

And I know you'd never go.

Not alone.

"Distraction"

Have you ever fallen in love as a distraction?

I have.

Many times.

Every time, I fear...

With him and with her...

Not always a favorite person.

I can fall in love with this thing or that thing.

Dancing.

Crafting.

Singing.

Telling jokes.

Sharing stories.

I can fall in love with a television show.

A movie.

A painting.

An album.

A city.

Anything to keep me connected to that feeling.

That desire to be seen.

To be heard.

To be represented.

And to be loved back...

I walk the borderline of my broken heart once again.

Tip-toeing around an unsavory truth.

I only know the kind of love that accompanies my illness...

And oftentimes...

It's a love that drives people away.

"Grace"

Fallen from grace...

And hitting the pavement with tact.

You always think that there won't be a next,

But then there always is.

Another blow to your ego.

Another notification from your old life.

Another reminder that it isn't over yet.

Thoughts and prayers to the girl who only knows how to fumble the ball.

She runs quickly, but she is clumsy.

I fear that she will never be alone.

Because they will always be there.

Watching.

Waiting.

What do you do when the distractions are never enough?

"You Found Me"

Always running.

Always hiding.

Always lying because I know that you watch.

You found me.

Now what?

Will you come all this way just to tell me that you hate me?

To demand more secrets after you told all of mine...?

What happens when you arrive?

Do you show up at my door with flowers in hand?

Do you tell me that you love me?

That you made a mistake?

Or does the charade continue?

Do you play the role?

The damsel in distress?

Afraid of the big bad bitch who left home...

To find solace away from you?

"Guillotine"

Heads will roll,

But not for you.

Because it didn't happen to you.

It didn't happen to them.

It happened to ME.

You should have known better than you to build your guillotine over a cracked foundation.

"Radio Tower"

Find me in the city.

On the rooftop where the radio tower glows bright and red.

Join me for a vial of poison.

There's not a star in sight,

But we can gaze at the planes.

"Fawn"

If misery loves company, then I'm in the business of company.

The Unholy Trinity awakens in me.

The Ghost of Reason.

False martyrdom...

And my God complex.

Caught.

Like a fawn in the headlights.

I stop in my tracks and face you head-on.

FLOOR IT.

For a people pleaser,

I know very few people who are pleased with me.

"Open Mic"

I spoke into a mic today and professed my love for her...

But I didn't mean it.

I lied.

For a joke.

It's crazy how my world has changed since I decided to walk away.

Cut the supply line.

Have you ever had a muse that you don't even like?

I have.

Her venom pulses through my veins

I quit acting for her... and for them.

I've performed for long enough.

I settle back into softness...

Safety...

Still triggered.

And absolutely swallowed whole by my own shame.

"Wallace"

Sometimes grief hits you like an avalanche...

And other times...

It hits you like that first gasp of air...

As you break through the surface tension.

"Stories"

Some stories are better told with time and distance.

I loved her.

Or at least I thought I did.

At first, it was the idea of her light.

Her creativity.

Her ability to paint in color in such a bleak world.

And then I met her darkness.

I grew to hate her.

And then I loved her more.

They say that if you love someone, let them go.

I couldn't tell you if I let her go because I loved her.

I'm not sure.

But I let her go when I knew that I could no longer care for her.

I saw her burn bright and Blue as she turned the city around me to ash.

And GODDAMN...

She was beautiful when she did it.

I meant it when I made my promise.

It's over.

It has been...

For a while now.

"Triduum"

Today is August 8th... 3 days from the big day...

Happy early birthday

To my biography born of bloodshed.

I don't know what to say...

You changed me.

For the worst.

And maybe...

Eventually...

For the best.

Will there be cake?

Yeah...

I'll have a slice.

After all,

It's my big day.

"Liars"

All of us are lying,

But some of us are better at it than others.

"Burn It"

I light the match.

Drop it on the ground.

A flame of Yellow erupts,

Nearly swallowing me whole.

Can a person you barely know break your heart?

She did.

And so did he.

I seek common ground,

But our common ground is shaky.

Always too much.

Never enough.

Every insecurity of mine deeply rooted...

In the sunflower field

Where The Haunted House once stood tall

Until it burned bright and Blue.

Yesterday, she returned.

New mask.

And a filthy confession...

One that crumbled the earth that I thought to be stable...

I gaze forward and just watch...

The flames dance in the wind.

Always performing.

Just for me.

"Grief"

You hate me to distract from your grief.

I love you to distract from mine.

"In Memoriam"

Here lies Cissy Stag.

Devoted wife.

Loving "mother"... of her peers.

Arsonist.

Cause of death?

Emotional relapse...

And smoke inhalation.

"Two"

2 days...

Happy early birthday to my biography born of bloodshed.

On days like this,

I kind of miss it.

"Overbearing"

Always too much.

Too mentally ill for the mentally ill.

Too intense for my own good.

Too traumatized to give other trauma survivors solace.

I don't want to heal.

Healed in this world means bland.

Bleak.

Uninteresting.

Sanitized

And I'm none of the above.

I want to fit in while standing out.

Poet.

Dancer.

Artist.

But how do I be any of THIS when I am so...

Unrelatable?

Friend.

Lover.

Colleague.

I fear that I have become too fiercely independent...

And it's isolating.

"Vodka Tonic"

I can still taste it on his lips.

The shame.

The pain.

He came running to my door,

And I was enthralled.

That was the beginning of the end.

"21"

Well...

Now 22...

22 poems written...

During an illicit affair

With a man I barely know...

What the FUCK, Cissy?

"Buried"

Sometimes...

Grief hits you like that first gasp of air...

As you break through the tension of the surface.

And other times...

It hits you like an avalanche.

Burying you beneath the cold and stone.

"Ice"

Sometimes...

Grief piles atop your chest like a sheet of ice...

That can only be warmed by old flames.

"Fall"

Have you ever tried to fall in love to distract from your grief?

I have.

The thing with falling in love with people is that sometimes... they do not love you back.

So, I wrote.

And I wrote.

And I WROTE.

MOUNTAINS of words that I could be proud of.

I reflected on my week.

My work.

And thought to myself...

THIS...

This is more rewarding.

"In Her Phone"

She shows me off the way that he shows her off.

"The Loneliest Girl"

Fake it 'til you hate it.

A smile on the face of the loneliest girl you know.

I am used to being chased...

But oftentimes... hunters do not know what to do once they catch me.

Especially if I let them...

"Batshit"

Soon, you'll be on the other side of the world...

And it still won't be far enough.

Happy birthday to my biography born of bloodshed.

You made me a star.

"Booby Trap"

I lay my trap and cover it in petals.

Who will fall this time?

I guess we'll see.

"Deal"

Your heart and soul be damned.

If you want to make a deal with The Devil,

You know where to find me.

"First Sight"

I loved you from the beginning.

From the first time that I heard you scream the F word from beneath your blonde hair and beanie.

From the first time I heard you play piano... and then play the same song OVER, AND OVER, AND OVER until it was the only song that I could remember how to play myself.

I loved you from the moment that you held me backstage and rocked me while singing in my ear.

I loved you from the first time I heard you scream that one song from SNL.

I loved you from the moment that we laughed together as we blew smoke into the air.

I loved you from the first wildly inappropriate sentence that you spoke to me.

I loved you from the first time that we watched your favorite TV show together, and I looked like the main character.

I loved you the first time that you gazed at me in fear with your large, brown eyes.

I loved you from the time we talked shit about the serial killer in your hometown.

I loved you from your first dirty joke.

I loved you from the beginning.

All of you.

I always have.

Even when I hated you.

Even when you hated me.

I loved you because made my life sparkle.

You made my stories worth telling.

And GODDAMN... you were beautiful when you did it.

"Ghost"

Here lies Cissy Stag.

The woman who lost her tether to reality...

And when she returned,

All the people were gone.

Her ghost roams this place in search of connection...

But her line has long been out of service.

"Projection"

It's the way that your stomach sinks.

At the sound of rapid footsteps.

You hope that you are wrong but know that you're not.

Why does it hurt so much?

When mirrors shatter and hearts break?

Because... what?

You saw your best qualities reflected in a person that you barely know?

Why are you so disappointed by them?

You still have you...

"Unfinished Business"

It's the way that the distractions just aren't enough.

Not in this moment.

How could I die if I am already a ghost?

I walk this earth with unfinished business.

Scaring the townspeople.

I found peace... and it was a bore.

"Aesthetic Perfection"

Have you ever searched for love in someone because they complemented your aesthetic?

I have.

His irises matched my headboard...

And that was enough for me.

He bared his heart, and I bared my body.

In the blink of an eye, I was hooked.

He was perfect.

On the surface at least...

He spoke, and I listened.

I quickly grew to know him,

And I knew that I wouldn't need to mirror him to match his soul.

But he didn't know me.

In fact,

He never even asked.

"I'm going to get him back."

The words that I spoke and knew to not be true.

That's all it took to send her running back to me.

Envious of my new muse.

Jealousy is a poison best served on the rocks,

And she's sipping on me at the bar.

I wrote this for the girl who lost everything.

At the hands of the woman with the beautiful life.

She carries my photo, and I carry her words.

This isn't what I pictured when I said that we were star-crossed.

"The Well"

People will see how far you have come since climbing out of the well that they pushed you down,

And they will tell others that it's dark magic.

She must be a monster.

A demon.

Not of this earth.

How else could she scale the walls from a bottom so deep?

Because I tried.

I never stopped.

I knew my value.

And I regained my power.

My safety.

My independence.

My voice.

My life.

By any means necessary.

Including sacrificing my identity.

Those who hurt you will whisper of your narcissism,

And sometimes, you just wink...

Because you know who you mirrored.

After all,

I was always a valuable student.

"When you know, you know."

And sometimes...

You just FUCKING know.

"Understanding"

It's the way that you screamed for so long.

See me.

Hear me.

UNDERSTAND ME.

And they didn't.

It's the way that your heart carried rejection after rejection after rejection.

Never good enough.

Your art.

Your work.

Your light.

You found darkness,

And they saw your value...

But they'd still never tell you.

And then... one day...

You blow up something new.

Out of fear.

You consider scheming...

Because it's what you've grown to know.

It's the only way to make them see your value...

You fumble the ball,

But you take the leap anyway.

You say you are sorry.

And you fucking mean it.

For the first time in a LONG time.

And they respond...

"I get it."

Inhale.

Exhale.

Safe.

You are finally safe.

"Miss You"

The hard truth is that I only miss her when I pick a fight with someone who I care about...

Because I'd rather fight with her than fight with them.

We're birds of a feather...

A rare pair that does not stick together.

"The Elevation Room"

The summer air smells like fall in the high elevation room.

I'm recovering from my high on him.

Summer flings aren't made to last.

Seasons change, and so do we.

I ponder my place...

And wonder what patience will bring to me.

This time... will I be happy?

Discernment is best served chilled...

But I've always liked my drinks hot.

"Shallow"

Daylight breaks,

And I am still grieving my identity.

The one that was stripped by a flame burning bright and Blue.

Replaced by the abyss of darkness that I now call my personality.

We're all mirrors.

Projections.

She projects her unmasked identity onto me,

And I project my unmasked identity onto him.

I swim from the deep end and finally begin to stand in shallow water.

I'm done treading.

The world outside of the pool is colorful.

So, I'm getting out of the pool.

"Vindicated"

And grateful that I don't have to see it.

"Yes"

It's the certainty in which you answer, "Yes!"

To the propositions that are not guaranteed.

Call it delusion.

Call it fate.

Call it what you want.

But I know what I want.

I always do.

"The Split"

I said it, and I meant it.

But I shouldn't have said it.

So, why did I say it?

I said it because I knew that it would bruise his ego.

I said it because I knew that he would fear me when he read it.

I said it because I didn't trust that he really understood me.

I said it because I got scared.

I said it because I caught feelings. Quickly.

I said it because I was conditioned to be a player.

I said it to keep him entertained.

I said it so that he'd think about me in my absence... because who fucking says that???

I said it so that he'd chase me.

I said it because I was insecure.

I said it because I felt safe... finally safe... and I forgot what safety feels like.

I said it because I didn't trust my own judgment.

I said it because it excited me to say it.

I said it, and I shouldn't have.

Because I could have waited to say it.

I had time.

"Teacher"

I don't spend my nights longing for her understanding.

Not anymore.

She was her own person.

Not an extension of my identity.

And for that, I am grateful.

Because I could never hate myself

As much as I hate her...

For everything...

I was always a damn good teacher,

And I meant it when I said it.

If you want to make it in this world,

You must adapt.

Learn the lesson.

"Packs"

I bared my teeth in your absence.

Lunged forward,

And drew blood.

Because I knew.

I knew that it was about you.

And you're not an extension of me.

You're your own person...

But in that moment...

I just fucking knew.

Call me crazy.

Call me devoted.

Call me when you want.

They say that we travel in packs.

I know my role.

And I always protect my own.

"Alter"

I frantically check my phone...

To ensure that my alter did not contact you...

While I was sleeping.

Learn from my mistakes.

I will.

I was conditioned to be a player,

And I'm done winning stupid prizes.

I wage this war with my alter...

She is jaded.

Always screaming.

And I am always screaming at her...

They will come to you if you just stop screaming.

For one. FUCKING. Second.

My alter and I join forces in this game of love and attention.

I shine bright, and she is the abyss.

Together, we are everything in between.

Make peace with my alter.

I will.

She is worthy of love too.

"Bitter"

Cut my coffee with lemonade.

I crave your bitterness.

Your tanginess.

Your sweetness.

Call it an odd mix,

But I know what I like.

"Hellraiser"

It's the way that you pulled your body from the rubble after you stopped seeing a future for yourself.

It's the way that you committed to your health.

To your healing.

To your voice.

To your narrative.

It's the way that they stripped you of your power...

Over, and over, and OVER again.

It's the way that you stood up for yourself.

Through your lies.

Through your truths.

Through your stories.

I never promised that I'd be a reliable narrator,

But I'm making damn good on my promise to live.

To entertain.

To recover.

To heal.

To move forward.

And to always show up as my most authentic self.

Cissy Stag, you are worthy of love.

Every part of you.

From your light as Melissa

To the darkness that you found in your alter.

You're going to make it in the business,

And you're going to make it in this life.

You always have,

And you always will.

"Glitter"

Am I broken enough for you to want to fix me?

Or am I beyond repair?

Has my glass been pulverized?

Do you look at me like I'm a glitter?

Do you whisper?

... you're beautiful... but...

I cannot put you back together.

"Choke Me"

On nights like these,

I feel sorry for them.

I lie in bed with a cerulean moon wrapped tight around my neck...

Tossing and turning at the thought of them.

I feel sorry for them because they chose distance.

Fear.

And for those reasons,

They will not know the pleasure of my presence on nights like these.

"Tranquility"

I turn the dial.

The silence is deafening.

I preferred listening to the radio when songs played.

"Flashbacks"

On days like this,

I am reminded of my trauma.

The tingling branches out to my palms.

I remember the truths that lie between lies.

Told for an audience.

I have nightmares.

About all of them.

Every hour of radio silence makes me feel like I fucked up.

Again.

Said the wrong thing.

Told the wrong joke.

Crossed a line.

Burned a bridge.

It's hard when your mind exists in paranoia.

In extremes.

You make yourself a martyr for a false cause.

If I didn't interfere... something devastating would have happened.

But you don't know that to be true.

You just know that you were worried.

How could you not?

Anyone in your position would have worried too.

"Like Me"

You liked me when your intensity made me nervous.

You wanted me when I feared connecting with you.

Tell me why when I stepped into my power,

And showed you a brave, new girl,

You lost interest.

Are you always hunting?

Have you never had a doe stop dead in her tracks?

Look you in your eyes?

And tell you that she will not he hunted?

We're equals.

So, let's call a truce.

You don't hunt me.

I don't hunt you.

And if we fall in love once the hunt is over,

So be it.

Tis the season.

"Sisters"

I gazed at the moon.

You're on the other side of the world,

But I wonder if you saw it last night.

It hit me for the first time as I paced home.

We don't fight like lovers.

We fight like sisters.

You - born to brothers.

Me - born alone for nearly 18 years.

I always felt a connection to you.

Like I knew you in a past life.

But maybe it wasn't what it seemed.

Maybe you were the petulant brat who babysat me and told your friends what a pain in the ass I was as you sang me lullabies and rocked me to sleep.

Maybe I was the little flea, always crawling under your skin, and telling all the school kids how much I adored my older sister.

In the haze,

I find clarity.

We were never made to be lovers.

Because in our last lives,

We were born of shared blood.

"Karmic"

I'd like a reading.

Pull from the deck.

Tell me that they are coming back.

They are just scared.

I know.

I was scary...

Because I was scared too.

Show me your cards and tell me that you're sensing karmic energy.

Someone with a substance abuse problem.

Big water to wine energy.

Cancer Scorpio Pisces.

A savior that nobody expected.

And nobody wants.

Tell me that there's a third party involved.

That's why they haven't come back.

In the tale of James, Betty, and August,

I fear that I am August.

Always have been.

Always will be.

"Score"

A poet's mind is a wild ride.

She called me a 6.5,

And she wasn't wrong.

Cissy means sixth,

And my tarot reader says I'm a 7.

You call yourself a 10?

Then baby, I'm an 11.

"Aurora"

I fear that I am losing my tether to reality.

I'm in the coffee shop,

Waiting for the show to begin,

Working on my site,

And sick to my stomach.

Yesterday was our anniversary.

You know the one.

Today is my half birthday.

And tomorrow is six months since I was taken into custody.

I begin creating.

Image after image after image.

And I imagine us,

Lying in the grass together,

In Florida,

Gazing at Aurora Borealis.

You're a terrible person...

But a perfect muse.

I don't want to love you.

I want to use you.

Back onto the pedestal you go.

I have art to create.

"Anniversary"

Fall used to be my season of love.

You changed that.

This fall, I will fixate on every date...

Every anniversary...

Of every tragedy brought to my life for your entertainment.

I dare not fall in love again this autumn.

As the leaves turn gold

And my world grows more beautiful.

Before the cold rolls in and obliterates every living being,

And I become the Ghost of Happy Christmas.

I hate you.

I hate you.

I hate you.

"Pills"

I pop a pill,

And feel my eyes sink.

Into my skull

Into my mind

And out of the world around me.

Fighting.

I'm always fighting.

Even when you aren't here.

The people around me are chatting.

Laughing.

Real people.

Drowned out by the voices in my head.

"One of the Boys"

I'm just like you.

Always competing.

Always angry.

Always hunting.

Always running.

"Full Moon"

What is it about the full moon...

That brings out the best in us...?

Is our blood moved like the pull of the tides,

Kickstarting our hearts to start beating again?

Between the loud I Hate Yous are the subtle I Love Yous.

All of us are lying.

Some of us aren't as good at it as we think we are.

"Climax"

Do you prioritize your pride over your pleasure?

Why?

Hurt egos only lead to hurt feelings.

Let me stroke your self-esteem.

Come with me.

Hold my hand and hike up the mountain.

When we get to the summit,

We'll start a fire.

Throw sugar in it and watch the flame briefly ascend towards the Heavens.

Descend into my wounded dignity.

Get my heart rate up.

We'll slow it down together.

In the afterglow of the climax,

We'll gaze at the stars.

Whisper about our lives – past, present, and future.

Our dreams.

Our desires.

I'll run my fingers through your hair before I kiss your brow.

You'll rest your head on my chest and hum sweet nothings.

Storm clouds gather above us in the night and extinguish our flame.

Neither of us move a muscle.

We're damp with sweat and raindrops.

All that remains of us are embers.

Inhale.

Exhale.

I've always loved the haze of a slow burn.

"Move On"

When you know,

You know.

I knew the day that I met you.

That was the day that I told him that I wasn't coming home.

I knew on the day that we became friends.

That was the day that I told him that I wanted to see other people.

I knew on the day that you broke my heart.

That was the day that I told him that I'd moved on.

When you know,

You know,

And I don't think you knew then,

But I did.

Call me uncool.

Call me crazy.

Call me intense.

Call me scary.

Call me when you want.

A lover.

A fighter.

A chaser.

A hermit.

Come out of your shell.

Join me in the ocean.

I've been to the bottom and back.

Trust me.

I know how to navigate the current.

"Monica"

I have a new reader.

Her name is Monica.

She tells me about my strengths,

My weaknesses,

My insecurities,

And she thinks that I write like Taylor.

Even better,

She tells me yours too.

We're all lying online.

I fear that I may be better at it than you.

"Use You"

You disarm me,

My mom and my therapist say that I'm going to break my own heart by allowing myself to stay fixated on you.

A muse is just someone to use,

But I'd like to use you for more than writing.

You keep me guessing.

Are you immune to my manipulations?

Are you running a play of your own?

Does it flatter your ego when you catch me drooling,

Or do I disgust you?

Do I frighten you?

Distance makes the heart grow fonder,

And I fear that I am unable to grow fonder of you as you remain distant.

For a control freak,

I'm ready to lose control.

Use you.

Consume you.

Touch you.

Love you.

Not the idealized version of you that I created in your absence.

You.

The real you.

Are you testing me,

Or are you uninterested?

"Get You Back"

I'm going to get you back.

I know exactly how.

You're a player,

And so am I.

And if I don't find love...

At least it'll be good for my career.

"Titanic"

Let's go on a date.

To the Titanic Museum.

I'll swipe my crappy, faux Heart of the Ocean necklace back from my sister.

Just for the occasion.

Put it on me.

Let's make a scene.

We'll stand at the bow of the boat and act out.

Just like Kate & Leo.

You'll scream, "I'm the king of the world!"

And I'll scream, "I'm flying!"

Our shouts will get lost in a sea of people.

Security will escort us out for disturbing the peace.

When we are out of building,

We'll laugh until our ribs ache,

And then we'll embrace,

And our lips will meet under an amber sky.

We'll have sex in the back of my Subaru.

You'll leave a print on the back window.

We'll listen to Celine Dion on the drive home.

"Dark Horse"

I have this fantasy.

You'll walk through the door of the tavern,

And find me downstairs.

With the band.

You sneak up behind me and put your hands in my front pockets.

We sway our hips together to the sweet lullaby of Sugar, We're Going down.

Afterwards, I run onto stage to cosplay Hayley Williams.

I scream my heart out.

Give you a show.

And then I leap from the stage.

We embrace.

Our lips meet.

You taste the tequila and soda on my tongue.

And in that moment...

The fantasy fades away.

You become as disappointed with me...

As I did with you

When you ran home to me

With the scent of vodka and tonic on your breath.

"Satisfied"

In this story of love, fixation, and idealization...

I think that we've hit a disruption in the plot.

In this moment,

I wonder to myself...

What if you're the steppingstone

To me loving her?

It sounds fucked up,

And I worry about how much it could hurt you...

But do you have what it takes?

To nurture her poetic soul?

To recognize her for the artist that she is...?

REALLY?

I mean... you didn't see it in me...

So, I struggle to believe that you saw her for her.

Truly.

Idealization.

Fixation.

Love.

Who is to say what's real?

But I fear that I may form a connection in your absence...

And I do not think that you will be satisfied.

"Irises"

Have you ever texted someone that you shouldn't have?

Just to confirm with their silence that you fell in love with the idea of them...?

Not the real them.

I have.

What a strange mind to live in...

Where one falls in love with the What Ifs,

But refuses to accept the Now I Knows.

I envision my life as a romantic comedy,

But my reality has become a romantic tragedy.

His irises matched my headboard...

And that was enough.

Enough for me to fixate on the version of him that I created in his absence,

And abandon my self-respect in the process.

"Home"

The tough thing about dating new people...

Is that they can all see how much I still adore you.

How much I respect you.

How much I love you.

Even if we're not together now,

And we never will be again.

I think that they find it unsettling.

When they come to my place,

And I tell them that I fell in love with this city...

Between the walls of The Highland Inn,

And that I spent my first night here with you.

Third floor.

Front of the building.

Back when the water ran brown.

You were there for me.

Always.

Through change.

Through loss.

Through betrayal.

Through the hardest times.

I love you forever.

You're home to me.

"Call It Quits"

When you know, you know.

And we both know that calling it quits was the right call.

Thank you for loving me for twelve... almost thirteen years.

We were once Amy and Rory,

But our dynamic changed.

If I'm Amy,

You're The Doctor.

Always my savior.

My rock.

Otherworldly.

And I'll always be your companion.

Eight months have passed since we called it quits...

But you're still there for me.

Tears flood my eyes...

Because I know that writing this poem doesn't mean goodbye.

No.

Not at all.

I wish you the best.

I always will.

And I'll think of you every fall.

"Better"

He said that he attracts crazy,

And I told him that I AM crazy.

It was the start of a summer fling...

That ended in sadness in only seven days.

I set my sights on getting him back...

And it didn't work.

He didn't come running to my door like that first intimate night.

He disappeared.

Completely.

I felt my self-esteem plummet.

Better.

I'll do better.

So, I did.

The same way I always have...

Through my art.

Through my words.

A published sequel and a sparkling 5-minute set of dirty jokes later,

I knew that I was better.

Better at being myself.

Better at my craft.

People will call an artist mad.

Am I mad, or did you just make me angry?

"She Said"

I asked Monica about us.

A few of us.

Lovers that never were.

Lovers that were but never will be again.

Soulmates never intended to be lovers.

She said that we have a special bond-

One that shines brightly across a vast constellation.

My gut is filled with sadness as I analyze her review of squandered connections.

We could have been great.

Partners.

Collaborators.

Friends.

More.

I know something that Monica doesn't though...

None of us trust each other.

And some of us...

Well... we trust each other a little too much for our own good.

"The Algorithm"

I'm getting better...

At my craft.

At analytics.

But I feel that I am becoming less relatable to humans by the second.

Always asking questions.

Always mining for answers.

The algorithm loves me.

I fear that she may be the only one.

"Don't"

I can picture it now.

We're standing face to face under an amber sky.

Inhale.

Exhale.

I'm ready to let go of being jaded by you.

We'll shake hands and agree to a redo.

Let's be friends.

Don't you dare pull me close and press your lips to mine.

I don't do casual.

I get too attached.

Let's start over.

Friends.

And if you pull me close...

If you embrace me...

Be prepared to fall in love.

So, don't do it if you're not ready.

I deserve better than the last time.

Do not hold me close.

Keep your distance.

Shake my hand.

I'll ask how your day went.

When you speak, I'll listen.

And then I'll tell you about mine.

Like friends do.

"Rabbit"

I can see it now.

No redos.

You call yourself a rabbit...

Monica says you're a tortoise,

But I had to tell her that you quit halfway through the race.

Maybe you are a rabbit.

Always rushing.

Tapping out after that first sprint.

Show me better.

Doesn't have to be your best.

I'll still have fun.

Pop the rosy glasses right back onto my face.

Here, have a pair.

I brought extra.

Pick up where we left off.

There are lows,

And there are highs,

And, baby, I'd go down to get you up.

Lift your spirit.

It might not last forever,

But I last a long time.

I always do.

"Overt"

What if I touch myself to the playlist of your dirty jokes?

Does that adequately stroke your ego?

What if I tell you about the disappointment I feel

When I receive another notification of someone who wants me...

And each time it isn't you?

Does that scratch the chin of your narcissism?

What if I say that I want you?

Only you?

Heart.

Mind.

Body.

Soul.

Now.

And later.

Have I been overt enough?

Is this the attention that you require?

What if I tell you that this time, I'm not lying?

Would you believe me?

Embrace me?

Unblock me?

Consume me?

Would you come with me?

"Dopamine"

In your absence, I've been running.

Chasing that high.

The one that got me hooked on you...

In only a sennight.

They say that it's difficult...

To move on from a situationship.

It's chemical.

"Hide"

His irises matched my headboard,

And that was enough for me to hide mine.

I always pictured it differently.

I'd look him right in his eyes.

Fearless.

Confident.

But it wasn't like that at all.

I'm the worst thing that a player can be.

A romantic.

So, I gazed down.

Slid the manuscript of my inner thoughts across the table,

And ran...

Shoot your shot.

I did.

And goddamn, did it scare me.

The ball is in your court now.

Don't fumble it.

"Vision"

"I'll see you when I see you," he whispered in my ear as I walked out of his door with my dignity intact.

My anxiety faded,

And my heart grew fonder.

Trust.

I trust you.

I'll see you when I see you.

"Meet Me"

It's hard to witness you fumbling the ball.

I made my pass with my heart on my sleeve and told you exactly what I needed.

They say that we show our true colors when we are intoxicated.

You keep showing me your bloodlust for my body.

I get it.

You want to fuck?

Let's just say that I don't fuck people who don't prioritize my needs.

I deserve better.

This time, I will not abandon myself.

Meet me where I am.

I didn't ask for much.

"Dried Flowers"

You're fragile.

So am I.

We're like a bouquet of dried flowers.

Preservations of the people that we once were before trauma siphoned our souls of all nutrients.

Sit with me while I sit with my discomfort.

It's what I need from you during moments that I cannot distract myself from my pain.

My grief.

My darkness.

Embrace me.

You don't have to tell me that everything will be okay.

We don't have to lie to each other...

Or to ourselves.

Your presence is enough for me.

"Dreams"

We tiptoe on the borderline of each other's boundaries.

Always testing how far each of us can go before the other pulls away.

Soon, you'll be in the mountains,

And I'll be in the city.

I'll tell myself every day not to grow anxious in your absence.

You have dreams to pursue, and so do I.

We have time.

"Sticky"

The worst thing about fantasy is that a version of it can exist if you're patient enough.

It's a shame that I've never been patient.

Pull me in.

Hold me close.

Consume me.

I've never been one to shy away from a sticky situation.

"Safe"

Trapped.

In The Enclosure built with my own imagination.

For a reader, I lack confidence in my ability to read you.

I see you through panes of glass.

You're RIGHT THERE.

I reach out to touch you, but I find myself unable to penetrate the barrier between us.

Let your guard down.

I won't coddle you,

But I'll take care of you.

I'm powerful.

I'm emotional.

I'm confrontational.

I'm strategic.

I'm a force to be reckoned with.

But when it comes down to it... I'm safe.

My love is worth the risk.

Because I always protect my people.

"Whinny"

If I'm a dark empath, he's a dark horse.

The unexpected winner of the heart of an underdog.

I heard him whinny in the night,

And I replied by howling.

"Death by a Thousand Strikes"

She was the death of my marriage.

One thousand strikes to my identity.

One thousand more to my sanity.

She plucked at my insecurities until I feared him... and he feared me.

She told me that I was delusional if I thought someone was out to get me.

But I wasn't. Because someone was. Her.

And then she told the world that my lovers hated me.

"I'm manipulating a man to get him back."

A half-truth that I tell an audience.

Because I don't have to manipulate my new muse to feel wanted,

But I have to manipulate her to ensure that he will be safe...

Should he ever become more than my muse.

I hurt your ego, and you came for blood.

Mark my words.

You will not come for my heart again.

Cross it, and hope I die.

That's what you wanted from me, right?

I wished you well,

And you wished me dead.

Forgive me,

For I cannot forgive you for the words that you said.

"People Like Us"

This time, I won't abandon myself.

I'll wear my heart on my sleeve,

And I'll trust that he is capable of handling it.

His irises matched my headboard,

And I saw how he looked at me as I walked through the door of the bar.

And before that... I saw how he looked at me as he told his dirty jokes.

And then... I saw how he reassured me when I expressed my fears...

That I'd implode the relationship.

They say that people like us fall in love with the ideas of people...

But honestly,

I think that people like us fall for people like us...

Because we can unmask around people like us.

And then we can be together.

Be honest.

And not self-abandon.

"Bouquet"

We're tactile creatures.

Always craving comfort through touch.

We're delicate and beautiful.

Like a bouquet of flowers with special meanings lying across a manuscript of soft, cream pages.

Memories of life, death, and rebirth.

I loved you in a past life.

I love you in this one.

I'll love you in the next one.

"Privacy Settings"

What a strange feeling.

To finally feel safe enough to grant myself privacy.

To spill sangria on my shirt and know that you have no idea.

That you're not here to prey on my insecurities.

That you can't see this to hurt me.

That you don't have access to hurt those around me as I pursue community. Acceptance. Love.

I showed you my cards.

All of them.

Love me.

Hate me.

Fear me.

Trust me.

And now... I can just float.

I don't know you anymore.

Barely did then.

"Highland"

September 2015.

I came here with my mom.

The water ran brown.

The black cat with the folded ear and large primordial pouch roamed the halls.

We ate next door.

And went to Piedmont Park to watch Elton John.

Nine years.

I can't believe it.

Now... it's home.

I'm home.

September 2024.

I've been here since December 2023

To escape the triangle where my trauma occurred.

'Tis the season for love and connection.

Inhale.

Exhale.

I love this song.

It reminds me of you.

"Pine"

There's always a song...

One that brings you back to your lowest point.

Oftentimes... it's a song that you treasure.

Just like this one.

I wake to a hazy morning,

And prepare to nurture my own soul.

Through art.

Through work.

Through nature.

Through music.

His irises matched my headboard,

And thankfully... I don't have to pine for his affection.

"Dear Jamie"

The flame that once burned Blue has long been extinguished.

All that remains of her is a wisp of smoke.

Floating in and out of the lives of anyone but me.

Thank God.

Dear Jamie,

I wish that I could thank you for my new life.

The city shines Blue.

But not for you.

For me.

You're on the other side of the world,

And it's finally far enough.

Today anyway...

I am safe.

I am loved.

I am home.

"Wine"

I wish that I was brave enough to say what I mean while sober.

What is it about vices that make you want to spill your heart out?

Bleed it dry where everyone can see it?

Tell a new flame that you adore them and then announce to your old flames that you're doing better without them?

I fear that the words will get lost with the other dark thoughts that haunt my mind if I don't say them.

Then and there.

But I'm not sure that they carry the same weight when I say them while drunk.

"Slip"

We slipped up last night.

Gave a subtle wink to each other's minds.

Exchanged energy.

I used to write to offer you peace.

And then I wrote to manipulate you...

To make you fall in love with me so that you'd finally respect me enough to listen to my screams.

We're addicted to chaos.

I know because we're addicted to each other.

I want to quit you like I want to quit red wine.

You intoxicate my thoughts like no other.

But I don't want you.

Not my lover.

Not my friend.

Not my enemy.

I want to be indifferent to you.

Break the bond and move on.

Unfortunately... I don't think that I ever can.

So, I'll write about it.

Acknowledge that it's there.

And live my life forming more stable attachments.

To people.

To places.

To art.

To music...

He asked how I ended up in Charleston... and I didn't want to tell him.

So, I kept it brief... and I said that I didn't want to talk about it anymore.

Because it was you.

And them.

And every person who told me that I was crazy as I held the receipts in my hands.

That's how I ended up in Charleston.

"Tiffany Circle"

Heartbroken.

Like every time that I leave the house that I bought with my husband and pass Tiffany Circle.

Dear Jamie,

Tell me why I still seek comfort from you after you ruined my life.

I fell in love with him.

Quickly.

And I called the love of my life to cry over him.

Just like the times that I cried over you.

You're an ocean away,

And tonight...

It's not close enough.

The others don't get it.

Hell...

I don't get it.

But I always wrote to you when I was lonely...

And tonight...

I feel lonelier than ever.

"Manipulation"

Fear in his eyes.

In response to a text.

A test.

A batshit statement

Coming from a place where I have no self-respect.

Always a game.

A play.

A test.

I'm a player,

And I'm the worst thing that a player can be...

Head over heels.

Don't test me.

Eventually, I leave...

And you become just like her.

A muse.

Someone to use.

Does that scare you?

Hurt your feelings?

Ha!

I get it.

I know how badly it hurts.

To be rejected.

To love deeply.

And hurt deeply.

All while trying to love yourself.

Find your peace.

Continue healing.

"Bite Marks"

Did I do enough to repel you for good this time?

I saw the bite marks on your neck,

And I knew that you had been sired by another.

So, I drank poison and proposed that we fuck...

Just so that I could see the horror on your face at my proposal.

Identical to the one you brought to me to rekindle our flame.

I died last year.

You cannot bleed me dry.

I walk this earth undead.

A predator.

A creature of the night.

Always stalking my prey.

Learning their weaknesses

So that if they bite me,

I can put them out of their misery quickly.

Did I do enough to repel you?

When I mirrored your movements?

Disrespected myself in the way that you disrespected me?

Is it enough?

Am I the monster of your dreams yet?

I love you because you're like me...

But I'm certain that you don't love yourself.

"Five Words"

"I love you, you idiot."

I might as well have said, "Hit me with your car."

"Dead Horse"

I have this fantasy.

I'll walk into the bar,

And I won't bother scanning the perimeter.

Because I won't care if you're here.

I'll order a drink and scream my lungs out.

Tequila and soda.

And on your tongue will be...

Not my business.

Not my problem.

And not a thought that crosses my mind.

I'd like to amend my statement.

I love you but...

I love me more.

By a landslide.

Cross my heart.

I already died.

"New Suitor"

Everybody, act cool.

A new suitor has entered the arena.

To the love of my life,

I hope you approve.

To my beautiful watcher and her handsome enough minions...

Tell the town my story.

Don't fuck it up this time.

To the archer who I asked to pretend not to know me...

Seriously...

Shut it.

And your aim sucks.

All is fair in love and war,

And this is both.

"Not Like Us"

He's not like us.

Easy to scare.

Unwilling to make art out of his pain.

Still mortal, I guess.

I told him that I was dark.

He should have believed me.

Most people don't make peace with their watcher...

But I did.

I'll see you when I see you.

Or never.

I don't know.

We have eternity.

It's better to be feared than to be loved.

I fear that may be true.

I no longer pray that you fear me.

I absolutely... unconditionally... do not fear you.

"It is though..."

You were once my favorite person,

And now I'm your favorite artist.

That must eat you alive.

You're so vain,

You probably think this poem's about you.

"We All Lie Online"

You're so bad at lying that it's cute.

But hey...

Whatever keeps your audience's eyes on you.

Your secret is safe with me...

And my audience.

"Fountain"

Find me.

In the dark.

Where the water runs clear.

Town square.

It's funny how heartstrings can become so frayed.

Am I okay?

I mean... yeah.

I survived a wildfire.

I can survive the burn from a candle.

Life trickles back into the stories that I once told from bed.

"Move"

I won't lie and say that it doesn't hurt.

It does.

Move on?

I haven't.

But I am moving forward.

That's the thing about me...

When I fall, I fall.

I mean... REALLY fall.

I won't say that it didn't hurt me to catch your gaze in my peripherals.

It did.

I wonder if I gazed back.

If I did, I wonder if you caught me.

I tried my best.

Kept my distance.

Retreated into a world of music.

I deserved better.

I haven't moved on,

But I am moving forward.

"Mediation"

Dead to me.

Like my nerve endings that suffer

Because of your watching eyes

And your stupid lies.

I told you not to kick the hornet's nest.

A hornet without a home will sting...

And you took my home.

You foolish. Fucking. Clown.

"Subliminal"

It's the love that you find in words unspoken.

Through images.

Through music.

Through movement.

We speak a secret love language.

Sharing.

I'm not supposed to love you.

You're not supposed to love me.

But what happens when one of us is circling the drain?

We let our guard down.

Put on a show.

Something grand.

Beautiful.

Meaningful.

With a slight nod that says

This is for you,

And you'll be okay.

"Flashbacks"

How many times can you grieve the same lost life?

I don't know.

I'll let you know when I'm done grieving.

She told me that she couldn't afford to get help.

Because of me.

After what she did to me.

From her place of privilege.

I carry the burden of a fucked-up mind.

And a hurting body

Because of her.

And them.

She's not my responsibility.

Wasn't last August.

Isn't now.

People sometimes assume a larger role in your life than they are due.

They put a responsibility on you that is not owed to them.

You didn't support my business.

You weren't my friend.

We didn't talk.

You didn't support me.

You met me once.

So why do you continue to shove the burden of your well-being onto me as if we fucked?

As if you didn't actively ruin my life?

"For Him"

What if I told you that I've been lying?

Every time that I take the mic,

And say that I don't want you coming back?

What if I just say it

Because I worry that if you come back

You'll use me again?

What if allowing you to return makes me question everything about myself?

What will I tolerate to be loved?

How much understanding is too much understanding?

What if I found better?

But only for a moment.

And that moment has come and gone.

What if I don't speak to you first the next time that I see you?

What if you approach me?

Embrace me?

Say you're sorry for your indiscretion?

For falling into a moment like mine?

And I say that I'm sorry for shouting before throwing up tequila and soda...?

What if my own illicit affair gave me insight into your world?

And suddenly... I understood why you pushed me away...?

All is fair in love and war.

This is both.

Let's get coffee,

And gaze at the skyline.

No poison.

Just us.

"Bravo"

The cat's out of the bag.

I can't say that I'm surprised.

I pinned you as a player from the beginning.

Game recognizes game,

And I play the game better than you do.

Let's be honest.

I don't envy her for fucking you when you're drunk.

I'm not jealous that the morning after, you texted me.

I pity you,

And I pity her.

Because I knew when you came to me with bite marks on your neck

That you still weren't happy.

Here's what happens to boys who fly too close to the sun...

They get burned.

Keep running.

I'm not chasing you.

"Mirror Me"

I don't chase.

I lead.

Come with me.

I'll show you my ways.

I already know that you'll mirror me.

People like you always do.

And sometimes...

That's the only time that you respect me enough...

To tell me your truth.

"Acting Debut"

You're cute when you're acting...

But you're even cuter when you break character.

"Powerhouse"

She asked me why I fell in love with him.

Well...

His irises matched my headboard.

And...

His worst qualities are just like mine...

Screaming to be loved.

We held hands and walked through the green.

The mud.

She was radiant.

A little bit scary.

And a little bit scared of me.

We agreed to take it slow.

We're both lonely.

In need of touch.

Conversation.

And all the things that make us feel human.

She's a powerhouse.

I can already see it.

And for once...

I'd like to release my power.

His irises matched my headboard.

And so did his.

But it didn't matter.

He didn't reciprocate the love extended to him.

And neither did he.

But Hell... she might.

She's brave.

She's fierce.

And she made sure to let him know that she was there with me.

"Show"

Better.

I'm doing better.

I know that it seems silly...

The way that I tell the world about every new love.

And every new heartbreak

Packaged into dirty jokes.

People watch and whisper...

About the girl who clearly has no diary.

Show up.

Show out.

I will.

Flash back to 30.

I didn't think I'd live long enough to chase my dreams.

But here I am.

Speaking with the booker.

5 minutes.

Clean set.

You got it.

I'll be back,

And next time...

I'll do better.

"Body Language"

Lonely.

Yeah.

I am.

I stare at the moon and think about you in your absence.

Do you think about me as you stare at your ceiling?

Do you dream about me when you close your eyes?

I'm a reader, you know.

I see your body language evolve out of my peripherals.

Feel your energy shift.

Mirror you.

You're a runner.

Well... so am I.

And I'm a Hell of a competitor.

I don't want to be chased.

I don't want to be hunted.

But I'll let you watch me.

Observe my body.

And get caught up in your head about what I'm thinking.

Want to break the tension?

Speak up.

Otherwise... I'll live my life without you in it.

And you can continue to watch.

"About a Boy"

Everything hurts.

It has for a while.

How do you move on once you've become fixated?

I'm not chasing you,

But I'm chasing a high.

A substitution.

Someone to curb my addiction.

I run to pretty people...

And for some reason...

I can't stop telling them about you.

Defending you in your absence.

The company I keep is a reflection of me...

And I enjoyed your company while it lasted.

"Intimacy"

My idea of intimacy is shifting.

Why am I here?

Because I'm lonely,

It's the easiest way to socialize,

And I crave touch.

But beyond that...

I crave deep, unmasked conversation...

About you

And about me.

Get to know my soul.

I want to know yours too.

Let's talk about our desires,

Our identities,

And all the ways that we are human.

"Repentance"

Why confess?

Because I'm drained.

I feel burdened by the games.

I feel frustrated with you for hoovering as I pursue new connections.

I'm drowning.

It's not fun to psychoanalyze you.

It's not rewarding for me to offer you reassurance.

It makes me feel like I will forever be trapped in your narrative.

I let you go so that I could move on.

Let me go.

I want to float away.

I want to find love in someone who knows how to properly care for me.

I want to obsess over them.

Consume them.

Admire them.

Love them.

Every part of them.

And I want you to know that when I write about them, I'm not writing about you.

Body Language.

Bravo.

Powerhouse.

Does it resonate?

Then I did my job as a writer...

Because you were not the inspiration for any of those pieces.

Farewell to my old muse.

When I write you...

Just know that it's because you became someone for me to use.

I tricked you into falling for me.

Preyed on your weaknesses.

But not your fears...

Not your paranoia.

I preyed on your capacity to love.

Because you hurt me worse than anyone ever has...

And it was the best revenge that I could think of.

Confuse you.

Show you the pieces of me that I knew would speak to you...

And let you question your intuition about me.

Study me.

Decode my words.

Look for special meanings in my work.

And allow you to spiral knowing damn well that I was off limits.

Game recognizes game...

And you saw it in me long before I saw it in myself.

I did not intend to manipulate you when I spoke up for myself last year...

But when you screamed in my face in March...

And I saw the movie that you made of me...

Yeah.

My actions were justified.

I didn't come for blood.

I came for you.

Mind.

Body.

Soul.

Consumed you.

And spit you out.

"One Day"

One day, you'll say that you're sorry.

Today is not the day.

I see you struggling to make peace with your demons.

With your actions.

And with everything you did to hurt me...

And how I let you go.

I burn bright, and all that remains of you is smoke.

Floating in my atmosphere...

Begging to be the flame in my heart again.

But you're not.

And I let you go so that I wouldn't burn out.

I love me.

That's why I defended you in your absence.

I love me.

That's why I showed you compassion.

I love me.

That's why I write about you in a way that you hope to be.

I love me.

That's why I write him like I write you.

Your humanity is not lost.

We joke about monsters...

But we really are just people...

With finite time.

Mortal.

"Music"

She asked me what kind of music I like.

This song... because of her...

And that song... because of him...

If there's one thing about me to know,

It's that I do not exit relationships without good music.

I walked into the bar.

I came to sing.

Saw him in my peripherals.

Tapped him on the shoulder...

Ready to forgive.

And he didn't move a muscle.

As if I didn't exist.

But I didn't take it to heart.

I know who I am.

I know my value.

And I learned long ago how to live...

How to love...

How to find stability...

Despite finding my identity in someone else.

Love.

Fixation.

Identity.

I accept all these things as my strengths...

My weaknesses...

They make my world less bleak,

More colorful,

And a Hell of a lot more interesting.

I'm okay.

For the first time in a long time.

And when it comes down to it...

I really like her.

Because she's not a placeholder.

She's unique.

And she's only scary to me because she's new.

"Hedonist"

If I could go back,

Would I unmeet her?

Absolutely.

He and I married on leap day.

2020.

By spring, I'd ordered my first pair of 8-inch heels.

Amethyst.

And I was hooked.

It was always easy.

He would spoil me.

Birthdays?

Heels.

Christmas?

Heels.

When I was sad?

Heels.

It hurt to give them away...

Because it wasn't just who made them...

It was what they meant to me...

When he bought them for me.

If I could go back,

Would I unmeet her?

Absolutely.

Because she was the death of my marriage...

And now...

She looks to me for reassurance in her own.

I loved him before we met...

And I'll love him until my dying day.

By then... she will be a ghost of my past.

A distant memory.

A story.

A muse.

Someone to use.

And I won't care if it turns her on to watch me suffer.

"For Them"

They are not like us...

But at their core...

They are like us.

They are in separation...

And they have been for a while now.

Since spring.

Between the lies and the mask,

I saw what she lost.

Who she lost.

Her ride or die.

Her confidante.

The tiny girl with red hair who came to her shows.

Her best friend.

Her everything.

Over you...

If we are being honest with each other...

I know why she is coming for me.

She is angry.

She seeks truth.

She seeks reassurance.

And I cannot provide that for her.

I didn't know her,

She didn't know me,

And I do not care for her like I (unfortunately) care for you.

You are my divine masculine.

I am your divine feminine.

And...

It doesn't mean that we are in love.

It doesn't mean that we should be together...

But here is what it means.

You are her karmic...

And I am hers...

And neither of us care for their well-being.

Their story.

Their narrative.

Because they don't know us.

But they know each other.

And they need each other.

So, this I beg of you...

Let them go.

Both of them.

Completely.

Block them.

Stonewall them.

Not for you.

Not for me.

For them.

I'm a reader.

And not just for you.

Trust your gut.

Trust me.

I don't need you to run a play on my behalf.

I'm strong enough on my own.

I fight my own battles.

I'm a warrior.

And right now... you can't be.

So, heal.

But what happens between them...

It shouldn't involve you.

Or me.

So, trust me.

And if you still can't do that...

Trust you.

Block them.

Do not say a word.

Let them find each other again.

Trust me.

It's what they need...

And I have no stake in the matter.

I'm just a reader.

"Echeveria"

Her hair matched my husband's,

And I was hooked.

We met in January.

During the lowest point of my life.

"She doesn't trust easily."

"She bats."

"She bites."

I knew from the moment that I saw her...

She's just like me.

The first time that I experienced an ideation,

I FLEW to Kennesaw to meet her.

An impulse.

A gut feeling.

A reason to stay alive.

I didn't even call.

In following weeks,

I volunteered.

Every Saturday.

Just so that I could see her.

I knew that she was the one.

February came,

And I became aware of a pending punishment.

One with a sentence yet to be determined.

So, I withdrew my application,

Returned her supplies,

And brought the non-returnables to Carolina.

For her well-being.

And it broke me.

In March, I sat before a judge,

Asking to go home to Atlanta.

A copy of my lease,

A copy of my driver's license,

And my volunteer hours accrued - all so I could see her.

My tether.

I returned to the rescue a few times...

But it was always hard.

My nervous system crumbled.

And there were days I couldn't move.

Like the last week.

When my husband and I signed the separation papers,

I resubmitted my application for her.

I found love in someone new.

QUICKLY.

And then Wally died.

And I fell to pieces.

In only seven days, someone new had come and gone...

And I just dissociated.

Completely.

And when I wasn't dissociating, I was sobbing.

Grieving.

The end of my marriage.

The loss of my boy.

And the loss of my life.

My home.

My identity.

My everything.

When I returned to the rescue, I was asked,

"Are you sure that she's the one?"

And I said yes.

While flirting with a few other suitors, of course.

She's been home for a month and two days.

For the first time, I gasped in a wave of grief...

And a river of tears in her presence.

And she was rattled. For two seconds.

She stood on my chest and kissed my lips.

I cuddled her,

And the moment of grief passed.

Sometimes, grief hits you like an anchor dragging you down to the bottom...

And other times... it hits you like the life saver tossed your way as you grow tired of treading water.

Love.

Fixation.

Identity.

I love her for her darkness.

And her light.

Always have.

Always will.

When you know, you know...

And I knew at first sight.

"Research"

I'm being investigated...?

Yeah.

I am.

I see you.

Running games on me.

To save me?

Help me?

Say you're sorry?

No.

I see you for who you are,

And I've been playing this game for a while now.

It turns you on.

When I flatter you...

And then scream in your face.

Who cares?

I'm not your type.

"Mirror You"

I almost did.

Stripped naked.

Bared my body.

And took a photo...

Just to censor...

And make you scream.

But then I looked into my own eyes.

Saw my reflection.

My beautiful body...

And thought to myself...

Damn...

You really fumbled the ball.

I'll save this for him.

Or her.

Or me.

Someone worthy of my affection on nights like these.

I see you foaming at the mouth...

Here.

Have a napkin.

"For Benny"

If I'm being honest with you...

The idea turns me on.

Just a tiny bit.

But if you met my conditions...

You showed up at my door....

Made an offer.

One that others couldn't resist...

I'd be tempted.

But...

I'd turn you away.

I'd tell you that it's for your own good.

But really... it would be for mine.

I tried tonight.

You know.

To come.

I could barely picture you.

It just... wasn't what I wanted.

And while it was fun to float the idea.

Tease you...

Think about you getting all up in your head...

I didn't come.

Because I don't want you.

She kissed my tattoos.

And my cheek.

Embraced me.

Introduced herself.

And told me that she loved me.

But we'd never met.

Not before tonight.

I flirted with her a bit.

Held her hand.

Tinkered with her fingers...

And when she wasn't looking,

I left.

No goodbye.

No number.

Nothing.

Want to know my most disgusting secret?

I'm a flirt...

With everyone.

But it's not that deep.

I'm waiting for someone who can meet all of my needs.

And I'm not sorry.

It's not you.

"Anti-Stalk Me"

Let's chat.

Lover to lover.

We're not in love.

We don't even respect each other.

But our values align.

I value your platform,

And you value my voice.

You're here anyway,

So, let's make the most of it.

Detach from everything that the internet says that we should be... what's right... what's wrong.

What do you want?

I know what I want.

To use my gifts to make the world safer.

For people like me.

And people unlike me.

Do your gifts feel too good to be true?

They are.

But I gave them to you anyway.

This is the shoe you've been waiting for.

The Pleaser that drops.

You are no good for me.

I am no good for you.

But I don't mind if you watch.

Mirror me.

After all, you've lived your life without a handbook...

And for the first time...

You are tip toeing in my Pleasers.

And I am running.

Towards my dreams.

Towards my goals.

Towards finding love.

In people and places and things that nurture my soul.

I worked hard.

I deserve it.

"The Table"

Do you feel the chill down your spine?

The tingle that reaches down through your fingertips?

Trails down your body...

And reaches down between your legs...

Power.

That's the feeling.

Don't get ahead of yourself.

Don't let it scare you.

The tables have turned,

And sex is on the table.

In your dreams, at least...

After all, I AM your FP.

Fantasy person.

When you take a lover,

Think of me.

Scream my name in your head.

But when you open your mouth...

Bite your lip.

Suppress it.

Until you gasp.

And if it's not enough...

Tell your lover,

"Choke me."

All is fair in love and war.

And this is war.

One where we all pull our weight.

Do our part.

And bask in the glimmers.

There are countless stars in the sky.

Sure.

But I'm not any ol' star.

I'm the sun.

You're the moon.

A reflection of me.

My mirror.

So, mirror me.

Do the work.

Do your part.

And if it gets you off...

So be it.

There is always collateral damage in love and war.

"Betty"

In her tale, I'm August.

She is James.

He is Betty.

I'm a reader.

For all of us

She is where she needs to be.

In my tale... I am Betty.

He is James.

And I hope.

Pray.

EVERY DAY.

That someone slips up...

And tells him...

Exactly what I want...

And what I deserve.

I am worthy.

"Blind"

I mirrored you last night.

Took a leap of faith.

And nearly flung myself in front of a bus.

Figuratively speaking.

Over a miscommunication.

His irises matched my headboard,

And that was enough.

Enough for me to remain fixated on him.

And sever every romantic connection in hopes of his return.

I was given a glimmer,

And it blinded me to reality.

I felt like a God.

And then...

I found out that I was wrong.

...

I'm the worst thing that a player can be.

Too many steps ahead...

And often ready and willing to play myself.

I was livid.

Ready to consume every being who crossed me.

Mind.

Body.

Soul.

Chew them up.

And then spit them out.

...

I mirrored you last night.

Stripped naked.

Bared my body.

For someone worthy of my affection.

A friend.

Because when I needed him most,

He was there.

And I told him before all of this went down...

I might be back.

I watched him quiver at the sight of my beautiful body.

Until he let loose the kind of moan that you suppress, as to not wake your roommates.

And then I wished him goodnight.

...

When the call ended, I put my clothes back on.

Hopped in a car.

And rode up to the bar in hopes of seeing you.

But you weren't there.

So, I mirrored you.

Gossiped about you in your absence.

Learned your deepest, darkest secrets...

And suddenly, I didn't feel so bad about everything that I did to you.

...

Everyone receives their karma...

And sometimes... their karma is me.

Fragile. Like a flower.

Unstable. Like a bomb.

In your absence, my heart grew fonder.

Of those who speak of you in your absence like those who speak of me in mine.

Because you hurt them.

But... my heart grew even fonder of you.

Because from the deepest... darkest parts of my mind...

My body...

My soul...

I understand.

And I know why you are the way that you are.

"Get to Know Me"

Come with me.

I want to show you my aesthetic.

The preview of my life.

Want to dive deeper?

Beyond my beautiful mask?

Get to know me.

It's easy.

I'm the Director,

And you've watched my movie.

See something of interest?

Ask me questions about it.

Or tell me what you liked about it.

Take what resonates,

And leave what doesn't.

I'm a reader.

But before that... I was a performer.

Show up.

Show out.

I will.

Because I'm doing better.

Even when I'm not the best.

One baby step at a time.

"Easy"

Come with me.

To the garden.

Let's walk hand in hand.

We'll tell each other dirty jokes.

Laugh together.

Because we're doing better...

SO much better than we were before.

I'll sing sweet nothings.

You can tell me fun facts.

And it will just be... easy.

"Encouragement"

Healing is dirty work.

A practice.

A commitment.

To your health.

To your narrative.

To your safety.

To yourself.

Acknowledge your triggers,

And bask in the glimmers of this life.

Healing is scary,

But you are scarier.

You got this.

"Quatre"

It's strange, you know?

To embody The Devil herself from the bottom of the well

Then rise above it all just to become a God...

And one day,

You're just a girl again.

A regular girl.

With a phenomenal story.

I couldn't tell you if there was any rhyme or reason for the last four years...

All I can tell you is that I'm glad this last year wasn't my final.

"Stop"

When does it stop?

When do the moments of solitude cease to feel like isolation?

When does home start feeling like home?

When does your heart and mind finally register it?

You're lonely...

But you're not alone.

"Closure (Reprise)"

A narcissist will reveal themself.

I guess we always do.

Machiavellianism.

Narcissism.

Psychopathy.

The Unholy Trinity that once laid dormant in me.

I survived the well,

And I didn't like the animal that it made me.

So, I decided to show up.

Show out.

Be myself.

100%.

But it didn't matter.

His irises matched my headboard, and that was enough.

Enough for me to tolerate mistreatment from his place of privilege.

He spoke the words to me that I asked him to say months ago.

During the second split.

I cracked a smile because my intuition was right all along.

He's not the love of my life.

Just an excellent muse.

Someone to use.

He spit his words of vitriol to me directly.

The covert words that he spoke behind my back while maintaining his mask...

And I'm glad he did.

Because today...

I know that I am free.

"Order in the Court"

His irises matched my headboard,

And that was enough.

Enough to let my guard down,

And tell him everything about what brought me to this city...

And how it never stopped.

I'm not in love with him anymore.

He became a muse.

Someone to use.

Until I put my trust in him.

His irises matched my headboard...

And he got caught using me.

So, I trusted my gut.

My intuition.

And I did what any reasonable person would do.

Create art...............

From my pain. From my anger. From my place of lived experience.

And it worked!

On this day...

I know that I am free.

"Never Again"

Sometimes, you show up and show out because it's another step towards your goals.

Even when you don't feel like it.

I cannot always mask my sadness when I give a set.

Sometimes, it pours all over a stage uncontrollably...

Even when I deliver the lines with ease.

It wasn't supposed to be this way.

I wasn't supposed to be alone in Atlanta forever.

But I feel that way right now.

Alone.

Empty.

Without a soul to trust.

And always sinking my mind...

My body...

My soul...

Into online spaces.

Because I feel so disconnected from real people.

How could I not?

Have you ever survived your greatest trauma...

Just to have a group of men exploit you for it?

I have.

His irises matched my headboard...

And it's going to take me a while to mend my heart after experiencing his betrayal.

When it comes down to it... I don't care what or who he loses because I spoke out.

He tried to take this from me.

Art.

Performance.

A reason to heal.

A reason to stay alive.

My freedom.

My safety.

My voice.

So... yeah... my anger?

It's justified.

In time, he will be nobody to me.

A ghost of past mistakes.

But for now...

He's the void.

Siphoning me of the little bit of life that I have been nurturing in my soul.

Get hotter and funnier...

I'll try...

But I may need to take my time.

After all, that's what I wanted.

Love.

Happiness.

Community...

And time...

"Love in the Modern Age"

What is it about love in the modern age that makes us INSANE?

If we'd met when we were young and crazy, would things be then as they are now?

Before the age of social sanitation...

Toxic positivity...

"Healing"?

Would we have been human enough back then to just...

Fall?

Deeply?

Passionately?

Without a thought or care in the world from those uninvolved?

Would things have been different?

I'm not chasing you...

But I'm also not running...

Want me?

Catch me.

I promise...

It'll just be... easy.

"Double-Edged"

I never doubted my capacity to love you.

The ground shakes beneath me as I learn to love myself again.

Happiness...

I thought that people like us could make each other happy...

And I think that we still can...

But if you only love me when I wear my beautiful mask,

Then you do not love me for everything that makes me me.

My darkness.

My anger.

My sadness.

My voice.

My power.

You only love me when you think that I love you...

Which is a bit of a double-edged sword for me...

Because I always love you...

For your light...

For your darkness...

And for every shade of gray in between.

"The Devil Watched"

Hell isn't what I thought it would be.

I always pictured it like they wrote in the prophecy.

A lake of fire.

But it isn't.

Hell is an endless field of little fires...

Burning while the souls scream, "CISSY! WHY WON'T YOU PUT US OUT?"

And there I stand.

Unable to extinguish the pain.

The whispers

For those around me who burn.

I bled myself dry.

There is no water left in my vessel.

I warned you in the summer.

I'm fragile.

Don't test me.

And then you did.

And now you're right here with me.

And her.

Burning.

Am I too hot to handle?

Hmm.

Perhaps you should have read the instructions.

And handled me with care.

I took my blood oath with her and ran to you.

I told you that I wouldn't lie to you... not unless I had to.

Crossed my heart with crossed fingers behind my back...

For good luck.

While The Devil watched us all.

About the Author

Cissy Stag is an Atlanta-based writer, stand-up comedian, and glitter heels maker. Her debut title is *Stripped: A Collection of Poems Written in Recovery.* Cissy is an alumna of Florida State University. She resides with the love of her life: a black rabbit named Echeveria.